GW00367625

How to Pass COMPUTER SELECTION TESTS

How to Pass COMPUTER SELECTION TESTS

Sanjay Modha

KOGAN
PAGE

For Neha

First published in 1994. Reprinted 1995.

The right of Sanjay Modha to be identified as author of this work has
been asserted by him in accordance with the Copyright, Designs and
Patents Act 1988.

Apart from any fair dealing for the purposes of research or private
study, or criticism or review, as permitted under the Copyright, Designs
and Patents Act, 1988, this publication may only be reproduced, stored
or transmitted, in any form or by any means, with the prior permission
in writing of the publishers, or in the case of reprographic reproduction
in accordance with the terms of licences issued by the Copyright
Licensing Agency. Enquiries concerning reproduction outside those
terms should be sent to the publishers at the undermentioned address:

Kogan Page Limited
120 Pentonville Road
London N1 9JN

© Sanjay Modha, 1994

British Library Cataloguing in Publication Data

A CIP record for this book is available from the British Library.

ISBN 0 7494 1424 3

Typeset by Saxon Graphics Ltd, Derby
Printed and bound in Great Britain by Clays Ltd, St Ives plc

Contents

Introduction

An increasing number of companies and other organisations now routinely use psychometric tests for selection purposes. As a result many more people are likely to find themselves being asked to sit a test.

However, significantly large numbers of candidates approach selection tests with a negative frame of mind and view these tests as an obstacle rather than an opportunity to demonstrate their true potential. Unfortunately, very few candidates, when invited to sit a test, come prepared to grasp the opportunity.

Candidates who prepare in advance are more likely to show their true skills and potential than those who turn up and hope for the best. The prepared candidate will approach the tests with a positive attitude, have a lower level of anxiety, be more confident and less prone to making mistakes.

The aim of this book is to make available to a general readership the strategies developed while preparing candidates for selection tests. Its objective is to assist candidates in preparing for computer selection tests. Over half the book is devoted to exercises that will help the candidate to practise.

Practice can result in significant improvements in performance. It also boosts confidence and helps individuals to cope with nervousness. It makes individuals less prone to mistakes and ensures that the test is approached proficiently.

Acknowledgement

I owe thanks to Mike Bryon for permission to use material previously published under joint authorship. In particular, I am grateful for his permission to use parts of this material of which he was the author.

Part One

General Information about Tests

Where masculine pronouns have been used in this book, it would usually be quite as appropriate to use either masculine or feminine. This stems from a desire to avoid cumbersome language, and no discrimination, prejudice or bias is intended.

Chapter 1

A Brief Guide to Tests

What are selection tests?

Selection tests, as the name suggests, are tests designed and used for the purpose of selecting and allocating people. The tests can be used in a number of situations; for example, in selecting for jobs, in promoting, transferring people to other departments, certain types of courses, career counselling or 'out placements'. 'Out placement' is a term used to describe a situation where a company wishing to make someone redundant provides help with finding another job. These tests are known as psychometric tests, also sometimes called psychological tests.

Psychometric tests are one way of establishing or confirming an applicant's competence for the job. They can be useful provided that they are *reliable* and *valid* for the job for which they are being used. Selection tests are standardised sets of questions or problems which allow an applicant's performance to be compared with that of other people of a similar background. For example, if you are a graduate your score would be compared with those of other graduates; if you have few or no qualifications your score would be compared with those people who are similar to you, and so on. This means that the tests are *norm* referenced (see page 16).

Are tests fair?

When we ask this question, what we are really asking is, do the tests discriminate against some people? The answer is yes. All good tests discriminate! That, after all, is their purpose. However, this discrimination should be on the basis of ability. This is fair and legal discrimination. If the tests, or the way in

11

which they are used, discriminate on the basis of sex or race then it would be unfair and possibly even illegal under the Sex Discrimination Act 1975 and the Race Relations Act 1976.

It does not matter whether the unfair discrimination is intentional or unintentional. The two types of discrimination identified by the Acts are direct and indirect. *Direct discrimination* is where an employer treats someone unfavourably because of his or her sex or colour or ethnic background. This type of discrimination is unlawful. *Indirect discrimination* is where an employer sets a condition which a large proportion of a particular group fail to meet, for example, women or people from minority ethnic groups. This type of discrimination could be held to be unlawful if the condition set by the employer is not necessary or justified by the circumstances.

However, the Acts do not explicitly refer to testing. The implication of the two Acts is that if the use of the tests (or other selection methods) results in proportionately more women or members of the ethnic minority communities failing the test and, as a result, their applications are rejected and the use of the test cannot be justified, this may be unfair discrimination. The onus of proof is on the employer to justify the use of the test.

To put it another way, if an employer sets a condition (for example, a test score of X or above) and a larger proportion of women or ethnic minority groups fail to meet this condition, compared to men or the ethnic majority group, the employer may be required to show that this condition is an essential requirement. If the use of the test can be shown to be justified, the result would be fair discrimination.

When an employer uses tests to select future employees, it is on the understanding that the test will differentiate between those candidates with the appropriate skills, knowledge and potential and those without them or at a lower level. Since a test which does not differentiate levels of ability in candidates is of no real value to the employer, it is important to the employer that the right person is chosen for the right job. It is equally important to the candidate that it is the right job for him or her. Otherwise the candidate may not be happy in the job; even worse he or she may not be capable of doing it, which can be very demoralising. In which case they may have to look for another job and go through the whole selection rigmarole again.

So we can say that fair discrimination is about distinguishing between people based on their abilities and aptitudes. However, these must be shown to be related to the job for which the tests are being used. What this means in practice is that if an employer uses a particular test to identify a given set of abilities and aptitudes, these must be shown to be necessary to do the job. For example, it may need to be shown that high scorers do well on the job in question and that low scorers do not.

Reliability and validity

Tests can be useful if they are reliable and valid. So what do these two words mean in this context?

Reliability

We can say that a test is reliable when consistent results are obtainable. For example, tests which contain ambiguous questions are likely to be unreliable because different people would interpret the questions differently or the same person may even interpret them differently on different occasions.

Validity

Tests are said to be valid when they measure what you want them to measure. In personnel selection terms it means that if it is to be of any use a test must be related in some way to the known demands of the job. For example, it needs to be shown that a test score predicts success or failure in a given job.

Figure 1.1 illustrates the kind of relationship that ought to exist between test scores and job performance, in which the higher the test score the better the performance in the job. In reality, however, it would be almost impossible to find such a high positive correlation. This is because of the difficulties in measuring performance in many, if not most, types of job.

To conclude, we can say that tests are fairer than interviews. The interview involves an interaction between the interviewee and the interviewer or interviewers (when it is a panel interview). During this process the candidate is being evaluated for his suitability for the job in question. This evaluation may be affected by personal prejudice, which may be subconscious, and social stereotypes.

Figure 1.1 *A positive correlation between test score and job performance*

Tests, because the examiners don't see who is taking the test, provide a safeguard against favouritism and arbitrary decisions. Therefore, when used properly, they serve an important function in preventing irrelevant and unfair discrimination.

Why do companies use tests?

There are a number of advantages to companies and other organisations in using psychometric tests, namely:

1. Where an organisation receives a large number of applications, and because most selection tests are of the paper and pencil type, applicants can be tested in large groups. This, of course, is much more cost effective than assessing the applicants piecemeal.
2. The recruitment and selection process can be costly, particularly if there is a high turnover of staff because of bad selection decisions or other disruptions. Thus, it is in the interest of the company to choose the right people for the job. The use of tests can help in this process, provided that the tests are both valid and reliable.
3. Tests can also reduce the subjectiveness in assessing the applicant's potential to develop his or her aptitude for a particular job. The lessening of the subjectiveness in the selection process is also an advantage for the applicants.

Test administration

Most tests are conducted under strict examination-type conditions. This is so that all candidates, at all times, are tested in the same manner, and therefore no group is either advantaged or disadvantaged in terms of receiving the test instructions or in the way in which the tests are conducted. For example, one group might be allowed extra time to complete a test and so have an unfair advantage. There is thus a high probability that this group's average scores will be higher compared to a similar group of people who did not have this unfair advantage.

The process that is followed will be laid down by the test publishers. However, the majority of tests are likely to be conducted in the following way:

1. All candidates will be sitting facing the test administrator.
2. Candidates will be provided with all the materials necessary, such as pencils, eraser and answer sheets.
3. The tester will explain the purpose of the test or tests and also inform candidates how the test will be conducted.
4. The tester will read the instructions that need to be followed for the test. These instructions may also be written on the test booklet, in which case the candidates should read them at the same time. In some tests the candidates are left to read the instructions by themselves. The reading time may be included in the test time or it may be extra. Whichever method is used, it is strongly advised that you read and understand the instructions. Experience has shown that many candidates fail to understand the test instructions and therefore make many errors in completing the answer sheets. For example, some tests may require you to fill in two or more boxes on the answer sheet.
5. There will be a strict time limit. For the majority of tests, if not all, there is a time limit to which the tester will adhere. The tester may use a stop watch; don't be put off by this. Interest inventories and personality questionnaires do not usually have a strict time limit, though candidates are asked to complete them as quickly as possible.
6. Many tests have example questions. In some tests the candidates are asked to attempt these, while others have them already completed. In any case, their purpose is to ensure that the candidates understand what is required of them.

Once again, make sure that you understand what you have to do. If you do not know what you are required to do at the example question stage, the chances are that you will not be able to do the test.

7. In most tests the candidates will be given the opportunity to ask questions. If you do not understand what is required of you, you should seek clarification. You should not feel intimidated about asking questions, no matter how trivial the question may seem to you. The chances are that there may be other people with similar questions who haven't plucked up enough courage to ask them. So the motto is – ask, you have nothing to lose!

Test scores

So far we have discussed a number of issues concerning the background of tests. But now we need to address the question of what happens once you have taken the test.

Naturally, they are 'scored', that is they are marked. Once scored, the correct answers are added together. The result is called a 'raw score'. If there is more than one test all the raw scores are noted. A set of tests is called a 'battery of tests'.

The raw score does not really mean anything on its own. This is because it does not tell us whether it is good score or a bad score. For example, let us assume that candidate A gets 30 questions right out of a possible 50. So candidate A has a raw score of 30. If the test is easy and most people who are similar to him would have scored around 40, A's score is bad. On the other hand, if the test is a difficult one and most of the other people would only have scored around 20, candidate A's score is a good one.

So, for the scores to be meaningful we have to compare the individual's score with that of a similar group of people. We will then be able to say that, compared to those people, this individual is either average, above average or below average. We make this comparison by using what are called 'norm tables'. Norm tables tell us how other people have scored on a test. The group with whom we would compare an individual's score is called a norm group and test norms are the norm group's scores. In a norm-referenced test the raw scores are compared with those of a norm group.

When did testing start and why?

The first standardised test of ability was produced in France at the beginning of the century by Binet. Initially, the tests were developed for use with children for diagnostic purposes. It was not until the First World War that testing for adults really began. These tests proved to be valuable in selecting and allocating recruits for different types of work in the armed forces and also for identifying potential officers.

During the Second World War further advances in selection methods were made. Once again the tests proved to be valuable in allocating different people to a variety of jobs or trades at different levels or grades. There were certain advantages in using paper and pencil tests in groups, and these are still applicable today in commerce and industry. First, it allowed a large number of people to be tested in one sitting. Second, it allowed the people to be tested under the same type of conditions, ie the physical conditions and instructions could be standardised. Third, people could be allocated to jobs or trades for which they had the aptitude rather than simply being rejected or allocated to jobs on the basis of a simple interview, which can be very subjective.

The use of tests in the two world wars played an important part in classifying large numbers of people. Since then tests have been developed and adapted for the needs of industry and commerce. Many organisations, particularly larger ones, now regularly use selection tests because of the advantages referred to above.

Chapter 2
Why Prepare for Tests?

It has been widely recognised that those candidates who have had experience of selection tests have an advantage over candidates who are facing tests for the first time. The experienced or 'test wise' candidates are likely to:

- make fewer mistakes;
- understand better the test demands;
- be more confident;
- cope with nerves;
- have developed a better test technique; and
- be more likely to pass.

To counteract the advantage enjoyed by the test wise, test publishers provide test descriptions that usually include practice questions. The idea is that the motivated candidate can practise on these questions and, therefore, have the same advantage as someone who has had experience of taking tests. The problem, however, is that there are nearly always too few practice questions for the candidate to prepare thoroughly with.

It is for this reason that this book has been produced. In the author's opinion test publishers provide insufficient practice material to allow candidates to polish their skills and abilities and so demonstrate their true potential.

You will find in this book lots of practice questions. They are designed to help you brush up the types of skill examined in selection tests. They will also assist you to become familiar with the kind of question and the exam type conditions which apply in selection tests.

How to practise

The best type of practice is carried out on material which is similar to the questions found in the real test. You should also try to get hold of material which allows you to practise on material under realistic test-type conditions.

To be sure that you have the right type of practice material you should read very carefully the test description sent to you by the employer. If you have not received one, telephone and ask if they can provide you with details of the test.

Often, the test will be divided into sub-tests, each of which may be separately timed and designed to measure a different ability. Make certain that you have practice material relevant to all the sub-tests.

If a section of the test is not covered by the material in this book, or if you want further material, you might obtain it from three other Kogan Page titles: *How to Pass Selection Tests, How to Pass Technical Selection Tests* and *Test Your Own Aptitude*.

It is important that you organise your study properly. You should aim to do in total between 12 and 21 hours of practice. When you sit down to practise make sure that you have a block of time, say one to two hours, when you will not be disturbed, so that you can concentrate on the practice material and do timed exercises without interruption.

When doing the timed exercises it is vital that you do not exceed the time limits. Otherwise you will get a false impression of how well you are doing. In the real test you will be timed very strictly; indeed, the test administrator will have a stop watch to time the test to the nearest second.

Furthermore, you need to concentrate on the skills that you are least good at. Try to be honest with yourself. If, for example, you are weak in maths then spend more time practising this so that you can build up your speed and accuracy.

The day of the test

Make sure that you have had a good night's sleep and that you are feeling fresh and ready to go. You should also ensure beforehand that you have the correct details of where the test is taking place and how to get there. Leave home in plenty of time and go to the toilet before the test. You will not need any pens or paper for the test as everything is supplied. However, take with you your spectacles or hearing aid if you wear them.

At the test, listen carefully to what the test administrator has to say. If you miss a point or do not understand something, ask the administrator to explain it. It is highly likely that you will work through some example (practice) questions before the real test starts. Don't worry if you get any of the example questions wrong as they do not count towards your score. Make sure, however, that you realise what you did wrong. If there is anything that you do not understand, ask the test administrator to explain it. Don't be shy as this is your last chance to have something explained to you. Once the test starts you will not be able to ask questions or get help.

Test strategies

During the real test it is vital that you do not waste time on questions to which you do not know the answer. If it is allowed, do all the questions that you find easy first. Then, if you have time, go back to any questions you missed.

In multiple-choice papers you are given questions which provide a number of suggested answers. Your task is to select the answer which you believe to be correct. If you are not sure which is the correct answer, it may help if you rule out the incorrect answers from the suggested list and then make an educated guess.

Make sure you indicate the answer in the way requested. Do not, for example, tick or cross out the correct answer if the instructions ask you to circle it.

If you are placing the answers on a separate sheet, check regularly that you are placing your mark in the correct place. If, for example, you are doing question 7 make sure it is against the number 7 on the answer sheet. A common error that many people make is that when they find a question difficult they move on to the next question, but they then mark the box of the previous question on the answer sheet.

Do not be surprised if you are not able to complete the whole test. It is quite usual for there to be more questions than it is possible to answer in the time allowed.

On the other hand, speed is of the essence, so work as quickly as you can without rushing. This is where practice can really help.

In multiple-choice maths questions estimating sometimes helps. Instead of trying to work out the exact answer to sums you find difficult, round the amount up or down to the nearest whole number.

Test anxiety

Do you worry a lot before taking a test? Do you tend to think you are not doing well while taking a test?

Test anxiety is quite a common problem for most people. The only difference is the degree to which people worry. Generally, it has been found that a slight amount of anxiety is a good thing, but a large amount is detrimental.

Too much worry and negative thoughts draw attention away from the task in hand, that of taking the test, and thereby disrupt performance. On the other hand, a little anxiety is beneficial; it will help you to be more alert and help your performance on the test.

If you are one of those people who worry too much and have negative thoughts about their performance during a test, you will need to learn to relax. You also need to be more positive. After all, failing a test is not the end of the world – though it may seem like it at the time.

What to do if you fail

Failing a test does not necessarily mean that you are incapable of doing the job or that you are not cut out for your chosen career. If you know what type of career you want, do not let a negative test result discourage you into giving up your dream.

If you fail, get some advice. Go to your careers office; the advisers are there to help you, regardless of your age. Try to find out about qualifications or courses which will help you to acquire the skills you need.

Apply to other organisations that recruit for similar positions. If they also use tests the chances are that you may do better in their test as you will be becoming 'test wise'.

Do lots of practice before you take another test and concentrate on the areas that you are weak in.

Chapter 3

The Most Common Types of Computer Test

Ability is the most common aspect of a candidate which is subject to testing, either in the form of paper and pencil or some practical exercise. These practical tests are sometimes referred to as performance tests or work sample tests. We shall talk about these later.

Ability tests fall into two main categories; attainment tests and aptitude tests. Aptitude is either having a talent for a particular skill or the potential to acquire it. The distinction between attainment tests and aptitude tests is not clear-cut. Therefore, a single test can be used to measure either attainment or aptitude.

Attainment tests

Attainment tests are those which seek to assess how much skill and knowledge an individual has. For example, an arithmetic test for cashiers measures attainment as long as it is used to measure arithmetic and not used to measure performance as a cashier.

From an employer's point of view an attainment test may provide a better assessment than simply looking at past records of achievements or non-achievements. A standardised test of arithmetic or spelling may give a more reliable indication of relevant present ability than a comparison of school qualifications in maths or English.

From a candidate's point of view an attainment test score will say more to an employer than simply talking about their skills.

This is particularly useful when the candidate does not possess many or even any qualifications.

Aptitude tests

Aptitude tests are used to predict the potential of an individual for a particular job or a course of study. However, as already mentioned, it is not easy to separate tests of potential from tests of attainment because all forms of test assess the person's current skills and knowledge. But the results of that assessment may then be used in a variety of ways, for example:

- to highlight the individual's strengths and weaknesses
- to provide career counselling
- to predict success in a job or course of study.

Work sample tests

Work sample tests can be described as a miniature version of the job in question. The tasks would encompass the major elements of a job. They are called work sample tests because that is the main purpose, and they are also practical. Hence they are sometimes referred to as performance tests.

Trainability tests

Another variation of the work sample tests is the trainability test. Trainability testing is a method of assessing applicants' potential for learning new skills in a particular area.

Tests of verbal reasoning

These are about how well you understand ideas expressed in words and how you think and reason with words.

Examples of the types of question that may be asked

1. Day is to night as sleeping is to _____ .

   (a) snoring (b) dreaming (c) waking (d) relaxing (e) not given

In this question you have to find the association between the first two words and then apply the same principle to find the answer for the missing word. The answer in this case is (c) waking, because night follows day and waking follows sleeping.

Fill in the missing word:

2. If you can see through something it means that it is_____.

   (a) opaque (b) transparent (c) vague (d) familiar (e) creative

---

The answer to question 2. is (b) transparent.

Tests of numerical reasoning

Like the verbal reasoning tests, the numerical reasoning tests aim to identify understanding of ideas expressed in numbers and how well you think and reason with numbers.

Examples of numerical questions

1. If five computer printer ribbons cost £40, how much does each one cost?

   (a) £10 (b) £9 (c) £8 (d) £7 (e) £6

2. If the sum of angles in a square is 360°, what is the size of each angle?

   (a) 60° (b) 70° (c) 80° (d) 90°

The answers to the above questions are:

1. (c)   2. (d)

3.

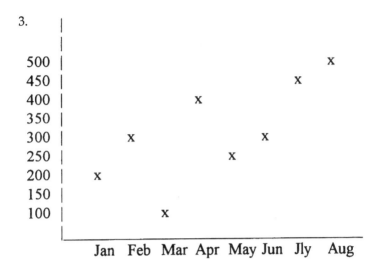

Car sales per month

In which two months were the same number of cars sold?

(a) Jan and Feb (b) Feb and Apr (c) Feb and Jun (d) Apr and Jun
(e) Apr and May

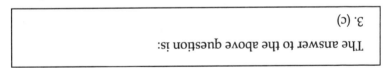

The answer to the above question is:

3. (c)

Tests of diagram reasoning

In tests dealing with diagrams, you will be presented with
shapes and patterns from which you have to work out a logical
sequence of events in order to answer the question. The format
of the questions is likely to be one where you are presented with
five shapes or patterns with one of the figures missing.
Underneath or beside these figures you will find a further five
shapes or patterns from which you will have to select one as the
missing answer. Look at the examples on the next page.

Examples of diagram reasoning questions

Question

1.
```
[]    []    []    ?    []
[]    []    []         []
[]          []         []
[]          []         []
            []         []
                       []
```

```
(a)   (b)   (c)   (d)   (e)
[]    []    []    []    []
[]    []    []    []    []
[]    []    []    []    []
      []    []    []    ][
      []    ][    []
            []
```

2. 0o0o0   o0o0o0   0o0o0o0   o0o0o0o0   ?

(a) o0o0o0o0o (b) 0o0o0o0o0 (c) 0o00o0o0o (d) 0o0o0o0o
(e) 0oo000oo00

3.

A   B   C   D   E

The answers are: 1. (a) 2. (b) 3. (d)

27

Other tests that you will find in Part Two of this book are:

- Tests using codes
- Tests using flow charts
- Tests of logic (putting events in a logical order)
- Tests using spreadsheets.

Chapter 4

Personality Questionnaires and Interest Inventories

Personality questionnaires

These aim to identify certain stable characteristics. Many people refer to personality inventories or questionnaires as tests. This is misleading, since to talk about personality questionnaires as tests implies that there is a pass or fail score, which obviously is not the case.

It would appear that personality is something that everyone talks about. One often hears people talk about someone having a 'great personality'. But what exactly is it?

There is no one theory or definition of personality with which all psychologists agree, but most personality questionnaires aim to identify certain stable characteristics. They are based on the assumption that the responses given will be a representative sample of how an individual will respond in a given social situation, particularly the one in which the selector is interested, that is the organisation or department in which that individual may be working. The main characteristics that personality questionnaires aim to identify in an individual are:

Extroversion	Introversion
Tough mindedness	Tender mindedness
Independence	Dependency
High self-confidence	Low self-confidence

Interest inventories or interest blanks

These aim to identify an individual's interest in particular occupations.

Strictly speaking, interest tests, like personality tests, are not tests at all because they are not about obtaining a good or a bad score, nor about passing or failing. It is for this reason that these are usually referred to as interest inventories or interest questionnaires. The aim of these interest inventories is to find out an individual's interest in particular occupations.

The interest inventories would cover interests in activities such as:

Scientific/technical	How and why things work or happen
Types of job	Different kinds of engineers and technicians
Social /welfare	Helping or caring for people
Types of job	Youth/community worker, nursing, teacher/instructor, social worker
Persuasion	Influencing people or ideas, or selling goods and services
Types of job	Sales person, manager, advertising
Arts	Designing or creating things or ideas
Types of job	Writer, clothes designer, painter
Clerical/computing	Handling data, systems
Types of job	Administrator, bookkeeper, computer operator, programmer, systems analyst

The use of interest inventories is limited, compared to say, aptitude tests, in the selection of applicants. This is because the inventories appear, at least on the face of it, easy to fake. For example, if a person is applying for a position as a clerk, then that person may deliberately indicate a stronger interest in tasks related to the office environment.

The interest inventories are probably most useful in vocational guidance where, one assumes, people are less likely to fake them.

Part Two

Practice Material

Chapter 5

Verbal Reasoning Tests

Exercise 1

1. Early is the opposite of _____.
   (a) night (b) morning (c) late (d) punctual
   (e) none of these

2. Wrong means the same as _____.
   (a) correct (b) right (c) answer (d) incorrect
   (e) none of these

3. Permanent is the opposite of _____.
   (a) temporary (b) secure (c) ever-lasting (d) faulty
   (e) none of these

4. Measure means the same as _____.
   (a) length (b) gauge (c) metric (d) weight
   (e) none of these

5. Vertical means the same as _____.
   (a) horizontal (b) sideways (c) upright (d) phobia
   (e) none of these

6. Aeroplane is to sky as ship is to _____.
   (a) dock (b) sea (c) navy (d) land (e) none of these

7. Long is the opposite of _____.
   (a) high (b) wide (c) short (d) lengthy (e) none of these

8. Repair means the same as _____.
   (a) amend (b) impair (c) destroy (d) mend
   (e) none of these

9. Problem is the opposite of _____.
   (a) obstacle (b) solution (c) query (d) difficulty
   (e) none of these

10. Foolish is the opposite of _____.
    (a) stupid (b) wise (c) modest (d) proud (e) none of these

11. Chair is to sit as bed is to _____.
    (a) lie (b) play (c) comfort (d) snore (e) none of these

12. Kilogram is to weight as kilometre is to _____.
    (a) ruler (b) speed (c) length (d) liquid (e) none of these

13. Hard is to soft as liquid is to _____.
    (a) drink (b) solid (c) water (d) defrost (e) none of these

14. Many is the opposite of _____.
    (a) several (b) single (c) few (d) some (e) none of these

15. Answer means the same as _____.
    (a) difficulty (b) easily (c) problem (d) solution
    (e) none of these

Exercise 2

In this exercise you are presented with a number of sentences. In each sentence you will find two or more words placed in brackets. Your task is to choose one word, by underlining it, that best completes the sentence.

1. All the guests (knew, new) each other at the wedding.
2. There was (to, too, two) much traffic at the main junction.
3. Louis was asked to collect the (draft, draught) from the bank.
4. To quote is to (cite, site, sight).
5. You should not switch (of, off) the computer until the disk has been removed.
6. Jane said her voice felt very (horse, hoarse).
7. Everyone went to the party (except, accept) James.
8. The postman brings the (male, mail) at 8am.
9. In the old days, water pipes were made from (led, lead).

10. The (whether, weather) forecast was not good.
11. The students found the test (quiet, quite) easy.
12. The electrical interference was (effecting, affecting) the computer.
13. She placed the disks over (there, they're, their) on the table.
14. The dealer (accepted, excepted) that there was a fault in the computer.
15. They were not sure (whether, weather) the problem was due to the program or the disk.

Exercise 3: The odd one out

	A	B	C	D	E
1.	Sun	Lamp	Candle	Moon	Window
2.	Plate	Cup	Saucer	Knife	Glass
3.	Pen	Pencil	Eraser	Quill	Chalk
4.	Dog	Cat	Whale	Salmon	Monkey
5.	Turkey	Ostrich	Eagle	Chicken	Emu
6.	Bus	Car	Bike	Sleigh	Waggon
7.	Horse	Donkey	Mule	Ox	Cow
8.	Phone	Fax	Modem	Telex	Television
9.	Table	Chair	Cupboard	Pedestal	Stool
10.	Water	Juice	Milk	Ice	Lemonade

STOP. Do not turn over the page. On the next page you will find a similar test that you should do under timed conditions. You will have three minutes to do the questions. When you are ready turn over the page and begin.

Exercise 4: The odd one out

Do the next ten questions under timed conditions. See how many you get through in three minutes.

	A	B	C	D	E
1.	Conceal	Hide	Obscure	Overt	Covert
2.	Feather	Beak	Fish	Egg	Nest
3.	Centimetres	Metres	Inches	Kilometres	Millimetres
4.	Squash	Tennis	Badminton	Table tennis	Cricket
5.	Novel	Short stories	Textbook	Exercise book	Tale
6.	Sheep	Cow	Goat	Cat	Pig
7.	Mat	Fat	Rat	Hat	Vat
8.	Red	Blue	Green	Colour	Pink
9.	Gallon	Litre	Pint	Quart	Fluid
10.	Taste	Smell	See	Hear	Cry

Exercise 5: Alphabetical order

On the left-hand side of the page you will find a number of
words. Your task is to rearrange the letters of the words in
alphabetical order. Place your answers on the right hand side of
the page.

Example question:

COMPUTER   CEMOPRTU

Now try the following ten tasks:

1. PRINTER   _____

2. DISK   _____

3. FLOPPY   _____

4. KEYBOARD   _____

5. SCREEN   _____

6. MEMORY   _____

7. SOFTWARE   _____

8. BINARY   _____

9. DATABASE   _____

10. EPROM

STOP. Do not turn over the page. On the next page you will
find a similar test that you should do under timed conditions.
You will have three minutes to do the questions. When you are
ready, turn over the page and begin.

Exercise 6: Alphabetical order

1. HARDWARE   _____

2. INFORMATION   _____

3. TECHNOLOGY   _____

4. LASER   _____

5. MAGNETIC   _____

6. MEGABYTE   _____

7. MICRO   _____

8. NETWORK   _____

9. SYSTEM   _____

10. PASSWORD   _____

Chapter 6

Numerical Reasoning Tests

Exercise 1

In this exercise you are presented with a set of numbers in a logical sequence. Your task is to find the sequence and fill in the missing number.

Example question:

| | 1 | 2 | 3 | 4 | ___ |

The answer is 5. The sequence in the above example is that the numbers increase by 1. Therefore the number following 4 is 5.

1.	2	4	6	8	___
2.	1	3	5	7	___
3.	1	3	6	10	___
4.	10	15	25	40	___
5.	5	11	23	47	___
6.	4	8	16	32	___
7.	10	5	15	10	___
8.	50	25	50	25	___
9.	15	11	8	6	___
10.	50	40	32	26	___
11.	100	75	25	–50	___
12.	150	100	200	150	___
13.	9	18	36	72	___
14.	1	2	4	8	___
15.	12	8	4	0	___

STOP. Do not turn over the page. On the next page you will find a similar test that you should do under timed conditions. You will have four minutes to do the questions. You should do the questions that you find easy first and then come back to the difficult ones if you have time. When you are ready turn over the page and begin.

Exercise 2

1.	2	6	—	14	18
2.	1	—	11	16	21
3.	10	20	30	—	50
4.	11	—	20	26	33
5.	2	4	16	—	65,536
6.	3	9	—	81	243
7.	1	4	—	64	256
8.	5	30	180	—	6,480
9.	80	40	—	10	5
10.	90	70	55	—	40
11.	6	—	18	24	30
12.	35	—	21	14	7
13.	20	—	16	14	12
14.	35	—	27	23	19
15.	37	—	23	16	9

Exercise 3

In this exercise you are required to carry out calculations. However, instead of numbers you are presented with letters. Each letter is given a value, but your answer will be in number format.

Let: A = 2   B = 3   C = 4   D = 5

Example question:

A + B = ?

In this case the answer is 5 because A = 2 and B = 3, therefore 2+3 = 5.

Remember that all calculations within brackets have to be carried out first.

Now work out the following:

1. A + D = ?
2. (A + B) – B = ?
3. (B + D) × A = ?
4. D – (A + B) = ?
5. (D × B) – D = ?

6. A + B + C – D = ?
7. (D + C + B) ÷ A = ?
8. (C × D) + (A × B) = ?
9. (B × C) – (A + C) = ?
10. B + C + D – A = ?

Exercise 4

Let: $A = 2$ $B = 3$ $C = 4$ $D = 5$
        $W = 6$ $X = 7$ $Y = 8$ $Z = 9$

Remember that all calculations within brackets have to be carried out first.

In this exercise you have to fill in the missing mathematical symbols, namely addition +, subtraction –, multiplication × and division ÷.

Example question:

$A ? B = D$
The answer is +. $A + B = D$ $(2 + 3 = 5)$

Do this exercise under timed conditions. See if you can do it in three minutes. Make sure you time yourself properly.

1. $(X + Y) = (B ? D)$ Ans_____
2. $D \times W = B \times Z ? B$ Ans_____
3. $A + Y = D + X ? A$ Ans_____
4. $Y ? W = A$ Ans_____
5. $Z ? D = Y \div A$ Ans_____
6. $A ? X = A + B + C + D$ Ans_____
7. $D + X + Y = Y ? A + C$ Ans_____
8. $W \times W + C = W \times X ? A$ Ans_____
9. $B + Y + Z = D \times Y ? A$ Ans_____
10. $X + Y + Z = C ? W$ Ans_____

Exercise 5

In this exercise you will be presented with numerical problems which are represented by letters. Each letter has been given a value which corresponds with its position in the alphabet. Thus A = 1 and Z = 26.

Give your answers as letters.

Example question:

A + B = ?

A = 1   B = 2   C = 3   D = 4   etc. Therefore A(1) + B(2) = C(3)

Hint. You will find it helpful to write down the alphabet somewhere and to number each letter.

1. F + ? = P	Ans_____
2. C + ? = J	Ans_____
3. L + D = ?	Ans_____
4. Z − B = ?	Ans_____
5. ? × K = V	Ans_____
6. C + D + ? = N	Ans_____
7. R − H = ?	Ans_____
8. P + A − G = ?	Ans_____
9. V + W − Z = ?	Ans_____
10. T × E ÷ D = ?	Ans_____
11. J × B ÷ ? = A	Ans_____
12. F × ? − J = Z	Ans_____
13. Y + ? − T = Z	Ans_____
14. R + P − L = ?	Ans_____
15. (C + D) × ? = U	Ans_____

For this part of the exercise please give the answers in numbers.

16. (P + N) × E = ?	Ans_____
17. (Z ÷ B) × L = ?	Ans_____
18. V + H + R − T = ?	Ans_____
19. (E × Y + Y) ÷ B = ?	Ans_____
20. T + (U ÷ C) = ?	Ans_____

Exercise 6: The binary number system

In the binary number system the only numbers used are zero and one (0 and 1). Computers use this number system.

Decimal to binary conversion table:

1 = 1	11 = 1011	21 = 10101
2 = 10	12 = 1100	22 = 10110
3 = 11	13 = 1101	23 = 10111
4 = 100	14 = 1110	24 = 11000
5 = 101	15 = 1111	25 = 11001
6 = 110	16 = 10000	26 = 11010
7 = 111	17 = 10001	27 = 11011
8 = 1000	18 = 10010	28 = 11100
9 = 1001	19 = 10011	29 = 11101
10 = 1010	20 = 10100	30 = 11110

Using the above table answer the following questions. Give your answers in binary.

Example question:

$2 + 2 = ?$

The answer is 100. The number 4 in binary is 100.

1. $2 + 3 = ?$ Ans_____
2. $2 \times 13 = ?$ Ans_____
3. $2 + 3 + 5 = ?$ Ans_____
4. $(30 \div 2) + 5 - 10 = ?$ Ans_____
5. $15 \times 3 - (5 \times 4) = ?$ Ans_____
6. $(16 \div 4) + (2 \times 2 \times 6) = ?$ Ans_____
7. $(30 - 10) \div (2 \times 5) = ?$ Ans_____
8. $2 \times 3 \times 6 - 15 = ?$ Ans_____
9. $6 + 7 + 3 + 1 = ?$ Ans_____
10. $(30 - 19) + 5 + 3 = ?$ Ans_____

STOP. Do not look at the next page. On the next page you will find a similar task. See if you can do it in five minutes (including reading time).

Exercise 7: The binary number system

In the binary number system the only numbers used are zero and one (0 and 1). Computers use this number system.

Decimal to binary conversion table:

1 = 1	11 = 1011	21 = 10101
2 = 10	12 = 1100	22 = 10110
3 = 11	13 = 1101	23 = 10111
4 = 100	14 = 1110	24 = 11000
5 = 101	15 = 1111	25 = 11001
6 = 110	16 = 10000	26 = 11010
7 = 111	17 = 10001	27 = 11011
8 = 1000	18 = 10010	28 = 11100
9 = 1001	19 = 10011	29 = 11101
10 = 1010	20 = 10100	30 = 11110

Using the above table answer the following questions. Give your answers in decimal number system.

Example question (the numbers given are in binary):

$10 + 10 = ?$

The answer is 4. The number 10 in binary is equal to 2 in decimal. Therefore $2 + 2 = 4$

1. $111 + 1001 = ?$ Ans_____
2. $1011 + 10 = ?$ Ans_____
3. $10000 + 10 + 10 = ?$ Ans_____
4. $10000 \div 10 = ?$ Ans_____
5. $(101 \times 100) + 1010 = ?$ Ans_____
6. $100 + 10 + 1000 = ?$ Ans_____
7. $(11110 - 1010) \div (10 \times 101) = ?$ Ans_____
8. $(1000 - 110) + (100 - 11) = ?$ Ans_____
9. $1000 \div 10 + (111 - 10) = ?$ Ans_____
10. $(100 - 10) \times (1001 + 101) \div 10 = ?$ Ans_____

Exercise 8: Constructing equations

In this exercise your task is to arrange the numbers and arithmetic symbols, presented below, to make true equations. You are then to choose a number from the list on the right that gives you a correct answer.

Symbols used are: plus (+), minus (–), multiply (×) and divide (÷)

Example questions:

1.　1　2　3　+　–　　　(a) 0　(b) 3　(c) 5　(d) 6　(e) 1
2.　2　3　4　+　×　　　(a) 20　(b) 16　(c) 12　(d) 10　(e) 8

The answers to the example questions are:

> 1. $1 + 2 - 3 = 0$　　The answer is (a).
>
> We could have written the equation thus:
> $3 + 2 - 1 = 4$　　However, this is not available in the answer list.
>
> 2. $2 × 3 + 4 = 10$　　The answer is (d).

Now try the following questions:

1.　5　3　1　+　–　　　　　(a) 6　(b) 5　(c) 4　(d) 3　(e) 2
2.　9　6　7　+　–　　　　　(a) 10　(b) 11　(c) 12　(d) 6　(e) 7
3.　8　4　5　+　–　　　　　(a) 4　(b) 5　(c) 6　(d) 7　(e) 8
4.　2　3　4　5　+　+　–　　(a) 3　(b) 4　(c) 5　(d) 7　(e) 9
5.　6　1　8　9　+　+　–　　(a) 9　(b) 10　(c) 12　(d) 14　(e) 16
6.　2　4　6　×　–　　　　　(a) 0　(b) 18　(c) 20　(d) 10　(e) 22
7.　7　3　1　×　–　　　　　(a) 1　(b) 3　(c) 4　(d) 7　(e) 21
8.　9　1　2　+　+　　　　　(a) 9　(b) 10　(c) 11　(d) 12　(e) 13
9.　1　1　2　+　–　　　　　(a) 1　(b) 5　(c) 3　(d) 2　(e) 4
10.　3　5　7　9　×　+　–　　(a) 17　(b) 18　(c) 28　(d) 24　(e) 60

Exercise 9

In this exercise you are required to find the missing number from one of the boxes. The numbers are in some kind of a sequence, and it is your task to find that sequence in order to answer the question. The sequence may be horizontal or vertical.

1.

1	?	5
2	4	6

(a) 1   (b) 2   (c) 3   (d) 4   (e) 5

2.

2	?	8
16	32	64

(a) 6   (b) 4   (c) 3   (d) 5   (e) 10

3.

3	9	27
?	243	729

(a) 61   (b) 90   (c) 81   (d) 101 (e) 141

4.

6	12	?
48	96	192

(a) 18   (b) 20   (c) 22   (d) 24   (e) 36

5.

2	20	15
4	?	30

(a) 10   (b) 40   (c) 8   (d) 16   (e) 18

Now try the next five questions under timed conditions. See if you can do them in two minutes.

Don't forget to time yourself properly!

6.

5	15	30
?	75	105

(a) 45   (b) 70   (c) 50   (d) 65   (e) 60

7.

1	6	12
19	27	?

(a) 35   (b) 40   (c) 46   (d) 36   (e) 34

8.

1	6	15
3	9	?

(a) 19   (b) 20   (c) 21   (d) 27   (e) 30

9.

3	12	27
7	17	?

(a) 37   (b) 36   (c) 34   (d) 33   (e) 31

10.

?	15	45
1	3	9

(a) 3   (b) 4   (c) 5   (d) 6   (e) 7

Exercise 10

1. If a computer company employs 500 people of whom 20 per cent are men, how many men work there?

   (a) 20   (b) 50   (c) 100   (d) 150   (e) 200

2. What is the ratio of men to women in the above company?

   (a) 1:2   (b) 1:3   (c) 1:4   (d) 1:5   (e) 1:6

3. Assuming that a dot matrix printer can print five characters per second, how many characters would it be able to print in two minutes?

   (a) 300   (b) 500   (c) 550   (d) 600   (e) 650

4. Three computers need different circuit boards replaced on each one. The cost is £125, £150 and £175. What is the average cost per board?

   (a) £450   (b) £350   (c) £250   (d) £150   (e) £125

5. If a computer floppy disk is able to hold 720,000 characters, how many characters would 10 disks hold?

   (a) 720,000   (b) 72,000   (c) 7,200,000
   (d) 14,000,000   (e) 14,200,000

6. A computer operator is able to input 120 characters per minute using a standard keyboard. How many characters can be typed in half an hour?

   (a) 360   (b) 3,600   (c) 36,000   (d) 1,200   (e) 12,000

7. If a set of 10 floppy disks costs £8, how much does each one cost?

   (a) £1.50   (b) £0.80   (c) £1.70   (d) £1.80   (e) £1.40

8. A woman buys a computer for £850, a laser printer for £599 and a mouse for £21. She gets a 10 per cent discount from the total price. How much has she paid?

   (a) £1,470   (b) £1,323   (c) £1,353   (d) £1,423   (e) £1,453

9. If a computer model A costs £600, model B costs 50 per cent more than model A and model C costs half the price of model B, how much does model C cost?

    (a) £600   (b) £900   (c) £550   (d) £450   (e) £700

10. If a customer chooses to buy the model A computer from the above question, what will the total price be with value added tax at 17.5 per cent?

    (a) £617.50 (b) £717.50 (c) £705.00 (d) £817.50 (e) £905.00

11. A businessperson buys 20 computers at a cost of £10,000. This person wishes to make a 30 per cent profit. How much should each computer be sold for to achieve this?

    (a) £550   (b) £650   (c) £750   (d) £675   (e) £700

12. A man is quoted prices for some software packages as follows: word processing at £105, spread sheet at £140 and data base at £135. There is a 10 per cent discount before tax. What would the price be after tax?

    (a) £401.85 (b) £501.85 (c) £446.50 (d) £380   (e) £491.15

Chapter 7

Diagram Reasoning Tests

In this test you will be presented with shapes and patterns from which you have to work out a logical sequence of events in order to answer the question. The format of the questions is likely to be whereby you are presented with five shapes or patterns with one of the figures missing. And underneath or beside these figures you will find a further five shapes or patterns from which you will have to select one as the missing answer. Look at the examples below.

Example questions:

1.

```
[]   []   []            []
[]   []   []            []
          []   []   ?   []
               []       []
                        []
                        []
```

A	B	C	D	E
[]	[]	[]	[]	[]
[]	[]	[]	][	[]
[]	[]	][	[]	[]
[]	[[	[]	[]	[]
	[]	[]		[]

2.

?

A   B   C   D   E

The answers are: 1. E   2. B

STOP. Do not turn over the page. On the next few pages you will find 15 questions. Try to do these under timed conditions. See how many you can do in five minutes.

1.

<o>	>0<		>0<	<o>
>0<	<o>		<o>	>0<
<o>	>0<		>0<	<o>
>0<	<o>	?	<o>	>0<
<o>	>0<		>0<	<o>
	<o>		<o>	>0<
			>0<	<o>
			<o>	>0<
			<o>	

A	B	C	D	E
>o<	>0<	<o>	<0>	>0<
<o>	<o>	>0<	>0<	<o>
>o<	>0<	<o>	<o>	>o<
<o>	<o>	>0<	>o<	<0>
>o<	>0<	<0>	<0>	>0<
<o>	<o>	>0<	>0<	<o>

2.

[V][∧][*]	[∧][V][∧]	[V][∧][V]		[V][∧][V]
[∧][V][∧]	[V][∧][*]	[∧][V][∧]	?	[∧][V][∧]
[V][∧][V]	[∧][V][∧]	[V][∧][*]		[*][∧][V]

A	B	C	D	E
[∧][V][∧]	[V][∧][∧]	[∧][V][∧]	[V][∧][V]	[∧][V][∧]
[V][∧][V]	[∧][V][∧]	[V][∧][V]	[V][∧][V]	[V][*][∧]
[∧][*][∧]	[V][*][V]	[*][V][∧]	[*][V][∧]	[∧][∧][V]

3.

4.

5.

6.

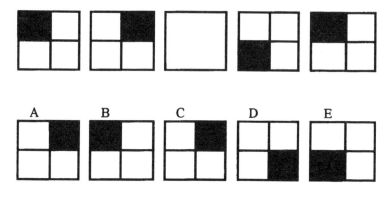

7.

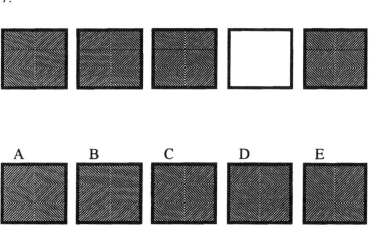

8.

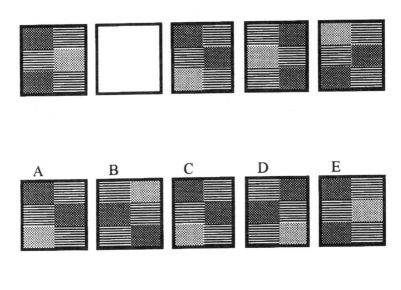

9.

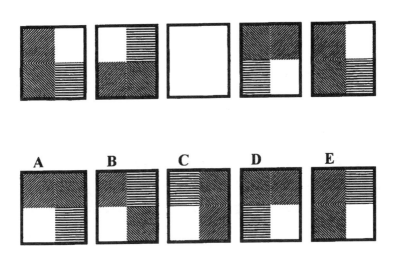

10.

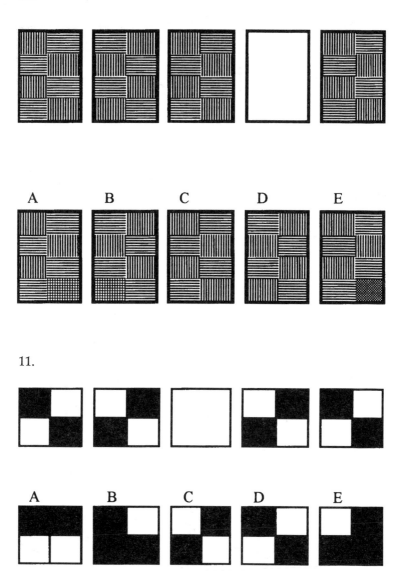

11.

12.

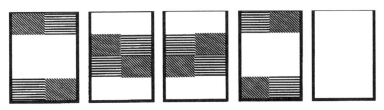

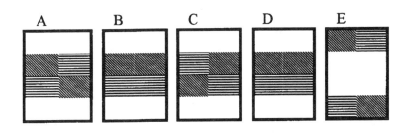

13.

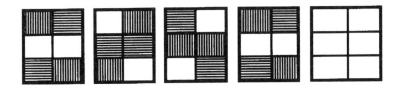

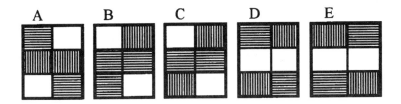

14.

QOQOQ   QOQOQ OQOQO QOQOQ
OQOQO   ?   OQOQO QOQOQ OQOQO
QOQOQ   QOQOQ OQOQO QOQOQ

A   B   C   D   E
QOOOQ OQOQO QOQOQ OQOQO OQOQO
OQQQO QOQOQ OQOQO QOQOQ OQOQO
QOOOQ OQOQQ QOQOO OQOQO QOQOQ

15.

?   { }{.} {'}{ } {*}{'} {.}{*}
      {'}{*} {*}{.} {.}{ } { }{'}

A   B   C   D   E
{.}{ } { }{.} {'}{ } {*}{'} {.}{*}
{*}{'} {'}{*} {*}{.} {.}{ } { }{'}

Chapter 8

Using Codes

Exercise 1: Coding and decoding

A = Z	B = Y	C = X	D = W	E = V	F = U
G = T	H = S	I = R	J = Q	K = P	L = O
M = N	N = M	O = L	P = K	Q = J	R = I
S = H	T = G	U = F	V = E	W = D	X = C
Y = B	Z = A				

In this exercise you are required to use the above codes to answer the questions. You will be presented with some coded words and you will have to translate them into proper words.

For example:

What do the following equal?

1. YZOO = _____. The letters YZOO = BALL. If you look at the letter Y in the above table you will notice that it equals B, Z = A and so on.

Now try the following:

1. BLF =	_____	7. TLG =	_____
2. SZEV =	_____	8. ZOO =	_____
3. WLMV =	_____	9. GSV =	_____
4. DVOO =	_____	10. XLIIVXG =	_____
5. RU =	_____	11. ZMHDVIH=	_____
6. BLF =	_____	12. VZHB! =	_____!

Exercise 2

Now code the following words. See if you can do them in four minutes.

A = Z	B = Y	C = X	D = W	E = V	F = U
G = T	H = S	I = R	J = Q	K = P	L = O
M = N	N = M	O = L	P = K	Q = J	R = I
S = H	T = G	U = F	V = E	W = D	X = C
Y = B	Z = A				

1. COMPUTER = _____
2. SCREEN = _____
3. DISK = _____
4. PRINTER = _____
5. MEMORY = _____

6. KEYBOARD = _____
7. DISK DRIVE = _____
8. DESK = _____
9. CHAIR = _____
10. PROGRAM = _____

Exercise 3: Using computers

Instruction	Code
To enter the computer	LOG/SYS
To use word processing package	WP
To use a database package	DB
To use a spreadsheet package	SPS
To create a new file	CF/NAME
To open and edit an existing file	EF/NAME
To delete a file	DF/NAME

Example question:

Which code would you use for the following?

To enter the computer and edit an old database file

Answer: LOG/SYS/DB/EF/NAME

STOP. Do not turn over the page. Over the page are eight questions of this type. See if you can finish them in three minutes. Don't forget to time yourself! Now turn over the page and start.

How to Pass Computer Selection Tests

Instruction	Code
To enter the computer	LOG/SYS
To use word processing package	WP
To use a database package	DB
To use a spreadsheet package	SPS
To create a new file	CF/NAME
To open and edit an existing file	EF/NAME
To delete a file	DF/NAME

Which code should be used for the following?

1. To enter the computer
   (a) sys/log
   (b) ef/name/log/sys
   (c) log/sys
   (d) on/com/pu/ter
   (e) none of the above

2. To delete a file from the database (assume you have already entered the computer)
   (a) df/namedb
   (b) db/df/name
   (c) df/name/db
   (d) df/name/sps/wp/db
   (e) none of the above

3. To enter the computer and create a new file on the word processor
   (a) cf/name/wp
   (b) cf/name/log/wp
   (c) log/sys/wp/name/cf
   (d) log/sys/wp/cf/name
   (e) none of the above

4. To edit a spreadsheet file by entering the computer first
   (a) ed/sps/log/sys
   (b) ef/sps/name/log/sys
   (c) log/sys/ef/sps/name
   (d) log/sys/sps/cf/name
   (e) none of the above

5. To delete a file from the word processing package
   (a) wp/ef/name/wp
   (b) df/name/wp
   (c) wp/cf/name/
   (d) df/log/name/wp
   (e) none of the above

6. To enter the computer and use the spread sheet program
   (a) log/sys/use/sps
   (b) log/sys/sps
   (c) log/com/sps/fa/st
   (d) log/sps/sys/name
   (e) none of the above

7. To log on to the computer and use the database
   (a) db/log/sys
   (b) log/db/on/to/sys
   (c) log/sys/sps
   (d) log/sys/db
   (e) none of the above

8. To use the word processor to create a file once you have entered the computer
   (a) wp/name/log
   (b) log/wp/name
   (c) log/wp/cf
   (d) log/wp/name/cf
   (e) none of the above

STOP. Do not turn over the page. On the next page is another timed exercise for you to do. If you need to have a break do so now, before you start the next task.

You have four minutes to do the next exercise. Don't forget to time yourself. When you are ready turn over the page and begin.

Exercise 4: Using computers

To enter the computer	LOG/SYS
To check database one	DBO
To check database two	DBT
To check database three	DBTR
To delete a file from a database	DF/ followed by the code of the appropriate database
To create a file in a database	CF/ followed by the code of the appropriate database

Which code should be used for the following?

1. To delete a file from database three (assume you have already entered the computer)
   - (a) dbtr
   - (b) df/log/dbtr
   - (c) df/dbtr
   - (d) df/dbo
   - (e) none of the above

2. To check database two (assume you have already entered the computer)
   - (a) dbt
   - (b) dbo
   - (c) dbtr/t
   - (d) dbo/t/tr
   - (e) none of the above

3. To enter the computer and check database one
   - (a) dbo
   - (b) log/dbo/sys
   - (c) log/sys/dbo
   - (d) log/sys/dbo/t/r
   - (e) none of the above

4. To create a file in database two (assume you have already entered the computer)
   (a) log/sys/cf/dbt
   (b) cf/dbo/t
   (c) cf/dbt
   (d) df/dbt
   (e) none of the above

5. To enter the computer and create a file in database three
   (a) cf/dbtr
   (b) cf/dbt
   (c) cf/dbo
   (d) df/dbtr
   (e) none of the above

6. To enter the computer
   (a) log/sys/dbo
   (b) log/sys/dbt
   (c) log/sys
   (d) log/st/ar/t
   (e) none of the above

7. To enter the computer and delete file in database one
   (a) log/sts/df/dbo
   (b) log/sys/cf/dbo
   (c) log/sys/df/dbo
   (d) log/df/dbo
   (e) none of the above

8. To create a file in database two and then delete a file in database one (assume you have already entered the computer)
   (a) cf/dbo and df/dbt
   (b) cf/dbt and cf/dbo
   (c) cf/dbt and df/dbo
   (d) cf/dbt and df/dbt
   (e) none of the above

9. To enter the computer and check database three and then create a file in database two
   (a) log/sys/dbtr and cf/dbo
   (b) log/sys/dbtr and cf/dbt
   (c) log/sys/dbtr and cf/dbtr
   (d) dbtr and cf/dbt
   (e) none of the above

10. To check database one, then create a file in database two and finally delete a file in database three (assume you have already entered the computer)
    (a) dbo/cf/dbo/df/dbtr
    (b) dbo/cf/dbt/df/dbt
    (c) dbo/cf/dbt/df/dbtr
    (d) dob/cf/dbt/df/dbtr
    (e) none of the above

Chapter 9

Other Tests

Putting events in a logical order

In this exercise you are presented with a list of events, but these are not in the correct order. It is your task to put the events in a logical order by writing the appropriate numbers in the boxes.

1. **Making a photocopy**
   1. Lift up the photocopier lid
   2. Press 'copy' button
   3. Close photocopier lid
   4. Go to the photocopier
   5. Place original on the photocopier

2. **Sending a letter by post**
   1. Seal envelope
   2. Post letter
   3. Write letter
   4. Go to the post office
   5. Put postage stamp on envelope
   6. Buy correct postage stamp
   7. Put letter in envelope

3. Boiling water in a kettle
1. Plug in kettle
2. Fill kettle with water
3. Wait for water to boil
4. Put kettle under tap
5. Turn off tap
6. Switch on power
7. Turn on tap

4. Applying for a college course
1. Fill in course application form
2. Receive invitation to attend an interview
3. Receive offer of a place
4. Accept offer
5. Attend interview
6. Wait for reply
7. Select suitable course to apply for
8. Read college prospectus

5. Using a telephone
1. Pick up handset
2. Wait for answer
3. Speak
4. Dial number
5. Put down handset when finished
6. Look up number in a directory

6. Going to work
1. Get on train
2. Get up
3. Go to platform
4. Get off train
5. Arrive at the other end
6. Leave home
7. Get to station

Using spreadsheets

A spreadsheet can be thought of as an electronic version of a piece of paper divided into a grid with rows and columns. Where the rows and columns intersect, that is known as a CELL. Each cell is identified by a reference number. The reference number is made up by using the letters along the top and the numbers along the side. Thus the first cell is A1. If you were asked to say where the number 64 appears you would reply, 'Cell D8'.

	A	B	C	D	E	F	G
1	2	4	6	8	1	3	5
2	10	12	14	16	7	9	11
3	18	20	22	24	13	15	17
4	26	28	30	32	19	21	23
5	34	36	38	40	25	27	29
6	42	44	46	48	31	33	35
7	50	52	54	56	37	39	41
8	58	60	62	64	43	45	47
9	66	68	70	72	49	51	53
10	74	76	78	80	55	57	59

Example question:

1. A1 + B1 = ? (The question is asking what the result is if you add the contents of cell A1 to B1)
    (a) G1
    (b) C1
    (c) E2
    (d) F2
    (e) none of the above

The answer is C1.

Now try the next ten questions.

71

1. A2 + B2 – C3 = ?

   (a) A1
   (b) B1
   (c) E1
   (d) F1
   (e) none of the above

2. D3 + A4 = ?

   (a) A6
   (b) A7
   (c) B6
   (d) B7
   (e) none of the above

3. C1 × A2 ÷ C4 = ?

   (a) D1
   (b) C1
   (c) B1
   (d) A1
   (e) none of the above

4. D2 × B1 + C1 = ?

   (a) A6
   (b) B7
   (c) C9
   (d) D8
   (e) none of the above

5. D10 – B8 + C6 = ?

   (a) D8
   (b) A9
   (c) C10
   (d) B7
   (e) none of the above

6. $C9 \times A2 \div G1 = ?$

   (a) F5
   (b) G5
   (c) A4
   (d) B4
   (e) none of the above

7. $(A7 \times E1) + (F8 \div G1) = ?$

   (a) E9
   (b) A8
   (c) F7
   (d) G10
   (e) none of the above

8. $(E4 + F4) \times (B4 - G4) \div A7 = ?$

   (a) G1
   (b) B1
   (c) D5
   (d) A2
   (e) none of the above

9. What is 10 per cent of D10 + B3?

   (a) A2
   (b) G2
   (c) A3
   (d) G3
   (e) none of the above

10. What is 20 per cent of D10 + D10?

   (a) B3
   (b) C4
   (c) D4
   (d) D8
   (e) none of the above

Alphabetical sequences

In this exercise you have to fill in the missing letter. The letters are in a sequence and you have to work out the sequence in order to find the correct missing letters.

Example:

1.   E   F   G   H   _____?

The answer is I. The letters are in alphabetical order and the letter after H is I. Now try these:

1.	A	C	E	G	_____?
2.	O	Q	S	U	_____?
3.	A	F	K	P	_____?
4.	J	L	N	P	_____?
5.	N	O	P	Q	_____?
6.	T	S	R	Q	_____?
7.	A	G	M	S	_____?
8.	B	M	X	I	_____?
9.	D	G	J	M	_____?
10.	Z	V	R	N	_____?
11.	A	B	D	E	_____?

Chapter 10

Using Flow Charts

Computers work by following instructions called programs. Computers follow each instruction one at a time. We can show how this works by using flow charts.

The following questions are described in the form of a flow chart. The flow chart consists of several rectangular boxes. These boxes contain instructions that need to be carried out. The boxes are joined by lines, which are referred to as flowlines and they indicate the direction in which the instructions must be carried out.

Some instructions are in fact questions to which the answer is either YES or NO. Boxes containing questions have two flowlines. You should follow the flowline which corresponds with your answer. For example, if the answer is YES you should follow the YES flowline.

You should also remember that instructions should be carried out in the order indicated by the flowlines.

By the side of each problem you will find a set of boxes containing numbers. For identification purposes the boxes have been labelled with letters. Look at the example below.

BOX LABEL	A	B	C	D
CONTENTS	1	2	3	4

We can see that box A contains 1 and box B contains 2 and so on.

When we carry out instructions such as 'put a number . . .' into a particular box, the new number replaces the previous (old) number in that box.

For example:

Put contents of box B in box C

This means that box C now contains the number 2 and the boxes will look like this:

BOX LABEL	A	B	C	D
CONTENTS	1	2	2	4

Note: the number in box B does not alter, and indeed all the boxes apart from box C remain the same.

Let us now look at some example questions.

Example 1:

	BOX LABEL	A	B	C	D	E	F	G
START	CONTENTS	1	2	3	4	5	6	~~7~~
Add contents of								6
box B with that of								~~10~~
box D and put								20
answer in box G								

Add contents of box G with that of box D and put answer in box G

Multiply contents of box G by 2. Put answer in box G

STOP

What number is in box G? _____

The answer is 20

The instructions can be written in an algebraic form. So we can replace

```
Add contents of
box A with that of
box B and out
answer in box C
```

by

```
A + B = > C
```

and we can replace this

```
Put contents of
box C in box D
```

by

```
C = > D
```

Example 2:

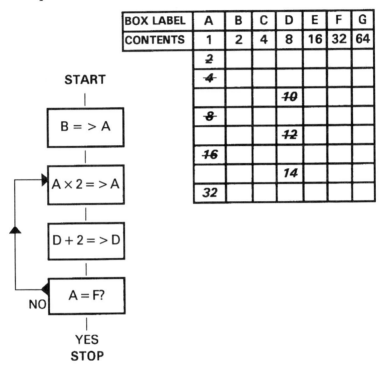

BOX LABEL	A	B	C	D	E	F	G
CONTENTS	1	2	4	8	16	32	64
	2						
	4						
				10			
	8						
				12			
	16						
				14			
	32						

START

|
B = > A
|
A × 2 = > A
|
D + 2 = > D
|
A = F?   NO
|
YES
STOP

What number is in box D? _____

The answer is 16

Exercise 1

Now try the following questions.

1.

BOX LABEL	A	B	C	D	E	F	G
CONTENTS	2	4	6	8	10	12	14

START

$A + D = > C$

$E + F = > G$

$G - D = > A$

STOP

What number is in box A? _____

2.

BOX LABEL	A	B	C	D	E	F	G
CONTENTS	3	5	8	4	12	9	6

START

C + D = > B

B × A = > B

B × 10 = > G

STOP

What number is in box G? _____

3.

BOX LABEL	A	B	C	D	E	F	G
CONTENTS	6	5	7	8	3	2	1

START

|

$A + B = > D$

|

$D \times E = > F$

|

$F - E = > G$

|

STOP

What number is in box G? _____

4.

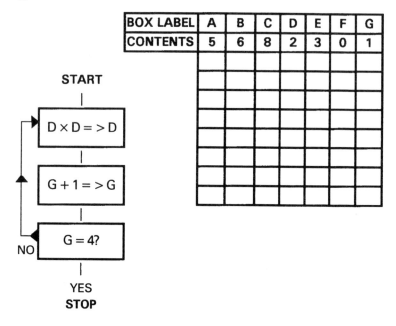

BOX LABEL	A	B	C	D	E	F	G
CONTENTS	5	6	8	2	3	0	1

START

$D \times D => D$

$G + 1 => G$

$G = 4?$

NO

YES
STOP

What number is in box D? _____

Exercise 2

Now see if you can do the next four questions in eight minutes.
Don't forget to time yourself!

1.

BOX LABEL	A	B	C	D	E	F	G
CONTENTS	8	2	3	4	0	5	6

START
|

$A => E$

|

$E \times F => B$

|

$B + 10 - 40$
$=> E$

|

STOP

What number is in box E? _____

2.

BOX LABEL	A	B	C	D	E	F	G
CONTENTS	2	4	6	8	10	12	14

START

|
| G × E = > A |

|
| F × C = > B |

|
| A + B = > D |

|
STOP

What number is in box D? _____

3.

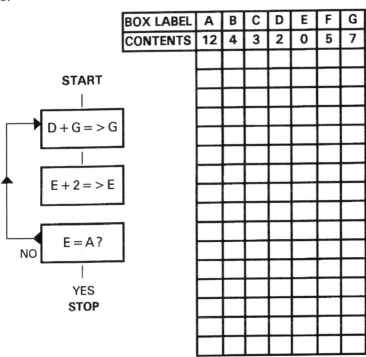

BOX LABEL	A	B	C	D	E	F	G
CONTENTS	12	4	3	2	0	5	7

START

D + G = > G

E + 2 = > E

E = A?

NO

YES
STOP

What number is in box G? _____

4.

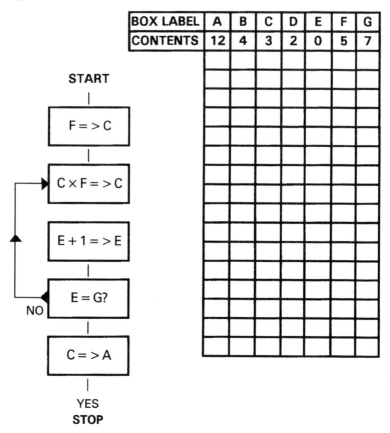

What number is in box A? _____

Chapter 11

Answers

Chapter 5: Verbal Reasoning (page 33)

Exercise 1

1. (c)	2. (d)	3. (a)	4. (b)	5. (c)	6. (b)
7. (c)	8. (d)	9. (b)	10. (b)	11. (a)	12. (c)
13. (b)	14. (c)	15. (d)			

Exercise 2

1. knew	2. too	3. draft	4. cite
5. off	6. hoarse	7. except	8. mail
9. lead	10. weather	11. quite	12. affecting
13. there	14. accepted	15. whether	

Exercise 3

1. E	2. D	3. C	4. D	5. C	6. D
7. E	8. E	9. C	10. D		

Exercise 4

1. D	2. C	3. C	4. C	5. D	6. D
7. C	8. D	9. E	10. E		

Exercise 5

1. EINPRRT	2. DIKS	3. FLOPPY	4. ABDEKORY
5. CEENRS	6. EMMORY	7. AEFORSTW	8. ABINRY
9. AAABDEST	10. EMOPR		

Exercise 6

1. AADEHRRW

2. AFIIMNNOORT

3. CEGHLNOOTY

4. AELRS

5. ACEGIMNT

6. ABEEGMTY

7. CIMOR

8. EKNORTW

9. EMSSTY

10. ADOPRSSW

Chapter 6: Numerical Reasoning Tests (page 39)

Exercise 1

1. 10	2. 9	3. 15	4. 60	5. 95	6. 64
7. 20	8. 50	9. 5	10. 22	11. –150	12. 250
13. 144	14. 16	15. –4			

Exercise 2

1. 10	2. 6	3. 40	4. 15	5. 256	6. 27
7. 16	8. 1,080	9. 20	10. 45	11. 12	12. 28
13. 18	14. 31	15. 30			

Exercise 3

1. 7	2. 2	3. 16	4. 0	5. 10	6. 4
7. 6	8. 26	9. 6	10. 10		

Exercise 4

1. Multiply (×)   2. Plus (+)   3. Minus (–)   4. Minus (–)
5. Minus (–)   6. Multiply (×) 7. Multiply (×) 8. Minus (–)
9. Divide (÷)   10. Multiply (×)

Exercise 5

1. J	2. G	3. P	4. X	5. B	6. G
7. J	8. J	9. S	10. Y	11. T	12. F
13. U	14. V	15. C	16. 150	17. 156	18. 28
19. 75	20. 27				

Exercise 6

1. 101	2. 11010	3. 1010	4. 1010	5. 11001
6. 11100	7. 10	8. 10101	9. 10001	10. 10011

Exercise 7

1. 16	2. 13	3. 20	4. 8	5. 30
6. 14	7. 2	8. 3	9. 9	10. 14

Exercise 8

1. (d)	2. (a)	3. (d)	4. (b)	5. (c)
6. (e)	7. (c)	8. (d)	9. (d)	10. (a)

Exercise 9

1. (c)	2. (b)	3. (c)	4. (d)	5. (b)
6. (c)	7. (d)	8. (a)	9. (d)	10. (c)

Exercise 10

1. (c)	2. (c)	3. (d)	4. (d)	5. (c)	6. (b)
7. (b)	8. (b)	9. (d)	10. (c)	11. (b)	12. (a)

Chapter 7: Diagram Reasoning Tests (page 51)

1. B	2. A	3. A	4. E	5. D	6. D
7. A	8. D	9. C	10. D	11. D	12. C
13. C	14. D	15. E			

Chapter 8: Using Codes (page 61)

Exercise 1

1. YOU	2. HAVE	3. DONE	4. WELL
5. IF	6. YOU	7. GOT	8. ALL
9. THE	10. CORRECT	11. ANSWERS	12. EASY!

Exercise 2

1. XLNKFGVI	2. HXIVVM	3. WRHP
4. KIRMGVI	5. NVNLIB	6. PVBYLZIW
7. WRHPWIREV	8. WVHP	9. XSZRI
10. KILTIZN		

Exercise 3

1. (c)	2. (b)	3. (d)	4. (e)
5. (e)	6. (b)	7. (d)	8. (e)

Exercise 4

1. (c)	2. (a)	3. (c)	4. (c)	5. (e)
6. (c)	7. (c)	8. (c)	9. (b)	10. (c)

Chapter 9: Other Tests (page 69)

Putting events in a logical order

1. 4, 1, 5, 3, 2
2. 3, 7, 1, 4, 6, 5, 2
3. 4, 7, 2, 5, 1, 6, 3
4. 8, 7, 1, 6, 2, 5, 3, 4
5. 6, 1, 4, 2, 3, 5
6. 2, 6, 7, 3, 1, 5, 4

Using spreadsheets

1. (e)	2. (b)	3. (d)	4. (c)	5. (b)
6. (e)	7. (d)	8. (b)	9. (a)	10. (c)

Alphabetical sequences

1. I	2. W	3. U	4. R	5. R	6. P	7. Y
8. T	9. P	10. J	11. G			

Chapter 10: Using Flow Charts (page 75)

Exercise 1

1. 14   2. 360   3. 30   4. 256

Exercise 2

1. 10   2. 212   3. 19   4. 390,625

Glossary of Computer Terms

Cross references are shown in italics:

Access time. The length of time between data being called for from a storage device, and the moment when it is ready to use.

Acoustic coupler. A device which converts digital signals to audio signals, so that data can be transmitted over a low-speed telephone line.

Alphanumeric. A set of characters which includes numbers, letters and other selected symbols.

ALU. *Arithmetic logic unit.*

Application package. A pre-written program, or suite of programs, which carries out a particular task, for example a word processing program.

Applications software. *Application package.*

Arithmetic logic unit. The part of the *CPU* which carries out arithmetic operations such as addition and subtraction, and logical operations such as the comparison of two values.

Artificial intelligence (AI). The capability of a device to perform functions that are normally associated with human intelligence, such as reasoning, learning and self-improvement.

ASCII Code. Set of character codes standardised under American Standard Code for Information Interchange.

Assembler. An item of software, usually supplied by the computer manufacturer, which translates a low-level language program into machine code.

Assembly language. A computer-oriented language whose instructions are symbolic and usually in one-to-one correspondence with computer instructions and that may provide other facilities such as the use of macro instructions. Synonymous with computer-dependent language.

Auxiliary storage. *Backing store.*

Backing store. Where large amounts of data can be stored, outside the immediate access store.

Backup copy. A duplicate of data or programs used to restore the original if it is lost or destroyed.

BASIC. This stands for Beginners' All-purpose Symbolic Instruction Code; a high-level programming language.

Batch processing. The processing of data accumulated over a period of time (ie batched) in sequence. The user cannot further influence processing while it is in progress.

Baud. A unit used to measure the speed of discrete transmission signals over a telecommunications line.

Bi-directional printer. A type of printer that prints in both directions, from left to right and the next line right to left, thus increasing printing speed.

Binary number system. A number representation system which uses the base 2 and which, therefore, uses only the two binary digits 0 and 1.

Bios. Basic input/output system. A computer's start-up instructions. They are held on *ROM* chips and are permanent in so far as they are not lost when power is switched off.

Bit. A binary digit.

Bootstrap. A program used to start (or 'boot') the computer, usually by clearing the primary memory, setting up various devices, and loading the operating system from secondary storage or *ROM*.

Buffer. A form of temporary storage which is used to compensate for the different operating speeds of the elements of the computer.

Bug. A defect or malfunction in a computer program or system.

Byte. A group of eight bits (plus one parity bit) which operates as a unit. One byte may hold one alphabetic or special character, or two decimal digits.

CAD. Computer aided design.

CAL. Computer assisted learning.

CAM. Computer aided manufacturing.

CBT. Computer based training.

CD ROM. Compact disk read-only memory.

Cell. Where a column and row intersect in a spreadsheet.

Central processing unit (CPU). The nerve-centre of the computer, which consists of the control unit, the *ALU* and the main store.

Chip. A tiny piece of semiconducting material which holds tens of thousands of electronic circuits (see *integrated circuit*).

COBOL. Common Business Oriented Language; a high-level computer language.

Compiler. A program that translates a high level language into the object or machine code of the target machine.

Computer. A machine or set of machines, controlled by an internally stored program, which accepts raw data and outputs information.

Computer virus. See *virus*.

Control unit. The part of the *CPU* which fetches program instructions from main store, interprets them, and then causes the other hardware elements to function.

CPU. *Central processing unit.*

Cursor. The flashing point on a *VDU* which indicates the current display position.

Daisy wheel. A print element for several popular printers consisting of plastic or metal disk with spokes radiating from the centre portion (like the petals on a daisy flower). At the end of each spoke is a circular area with a typeface impression on it.

Database. A consolidated file which holds the data relating either to the whole of an organisation's operations or the data relating to a major operational area. Databases are also known as data banks; they utilise the concept of the integrated file.

Data capture. The gathering of data at its source for direct input to a computer system.

Data collection. The gathering together of data prior to its input to a computer system.

Data item. The smallest element of data stored or used by a program.

Data pad. A pressure-sensitive pad which allows a user to write on a blank form and, thereby, enter data into a computer.

Data processing. Operations performed on raw data in order to produce meaningful information.

Data Protection Act. Introduced in 1984 to give certain rights to individuals, such as access to information held on computer.

Data Protection Registrar. Person responsible for maintaining a register of companies who hold information about people on computer.

Debug. The process of detecting and eliminating errors in a program or a system.

Dedicated word processor. A machine that can be used only as a word processor, it cannot run other programs such as spreadsheets or databases, as can a general purpose computer.

Desk-top publishing. Computer-aided publishing that uses equipment small enough to fit on a desktop or table and suitable for an end user. Also referred to as DTP.

Diagnostic program. A program designed to detect and locate faults in a program or system.

Dialogue. In a *wimp* environment, a small on-screen box that invites the user to enter a response to a query, an option, or other information.

Directory. A named, grouping of files on a disk that is recognised by the operating system.

Disk. A flat, circular plate with a magnetisable surface layer on which data can be stored by magnetic recording.

Disk drive. A device that houses a disk or diskette while it is in use. It contains a motor and one or more magnetic heads to read and write data on the disk.

Diskette. Synonymous with floppy *disk*.

DOS. A program which controls the flow and location of information between and in the various storage devices in the computer (Disk Operating System).

Dot matrix printer. A printer or a plotter that prints characters or line images that are represented by dots. Synonymous with matrix printer.

Double density disk. A disk which can hold twice as much information as a single density disk.

Double-sided disk. A disk which can hold information an both sides.

Down time. The length of time for which a computer system cannot be used due to a malfunction, or to maintenance being carried out.

Dry run. A process of checking the logic of a computer program by hand and off-line.

DTP. *Desk-top publishing.*

Electronic mail. A communication system for transmitting messages between computer terminals (E mail). There is usually a 'mail box' where messages are stored until retrieved.

Encryption. A method of encoding data so that it is meaningless to those who do not have a decoder.

End users. People who ultimately use application software.

EPROM. An erasable *PROM.*

Ergonomics. The science of designing, among other things, computer hardware and software to make them more easy and comfortable for users.

Error. A mistake or a fault that prevents the program or system from running as expected.

Error message. Indicates that an error has occurred.

Expansion board. A printed circuit board that accommodates extra components for the purpose of expanding the capabilities of a computer.

Expansion slot. A slot for installing additional expansion boards that perform functions not provided by the computer's standard hardware.

Expert system. Systems that can input data by the use of an expert knowledge base and a set of rules to reach a conclusion.

Field. On a data medium or in storage, a specified area used for a particular class of data; for example, a group of character positions used to enter or display wage rates on a screen.

Fifth generation computers. The computer that will succeed the current generation of computers. The term is understandably vague, but such computers are likely to be much faster and make greater use of *parallel processing*.

File. A set of related records treated as a unit, for example, in stock control, a file could consist of a set of invoices.

Firmware. Permanent circuitry such as dedicated *ROM.*

Floppy disk. See *disk.*

Flow chart. A graphical representation in which symbols are used to represent such things as operations, data, flow direction, and equipment for the definition, analysis, or solution of a problem. Synonymous with flow diagram.

Font. A family or assortment of characters of a given size and style: for example, Times Roman. Also fount.

Font cartridge. A cartridge that can be plugged in to a printer to increase or add new fonts to a printer.

Formatting (a disk). This puts the magnetic track and sector pattern on a disk, which is needed before the disk can store any information. Formatting completely erases any previously stored data.

FORTRAN. Formula Translation, a programming language primarily used to express computer programs by arithmetic formulas.

Fourth generation language. A flexible application development tool, such as an electronic spreadsheet, query language, or application generator, which allows you to develop an application by describing to the computer what you want rather than programming it in a how-to, step-by-step fashion. Thus it allows the user to tell the computer what to do, rather than how to do it.

Front-end processor (FEP). A computer configuration where the minor jobs or communication tasks are first processed by a mini-*CPU*, before transmitting them to the main CPU which handles all main batch jobs and programs.

Gigabyte. One billion (10^9) bytes.

Grandparent-parent-child backup. A file backup system in which the current version and the two previous versions of a file are always retained.

Hacker. A person who attempts or is interested in breaking into secure computer systems. Hacking is a criminal activity.

Hard copy. A printed copy of machine output in a visually readable form; for example, printed reports, listings, documents and summaries.

Hard disk. Rapid magnetic disk used for storing information, similar to a floppy disk, but has greater capacity and is housed inside the computer.

Hardware. The mechanical and electronic devices that make up a computer. See *software*.

High-density disk. A floppy disk that is able to hold a greater amount of information than a double-sided disk.

Icon. A small pictorial symbol in a *wimp* environment, representing a program option, which can be selected by clicking on it with a mouse.

Impact printer. A printer which uses some sort of physical contact with the paper, eg dot matrix printer.

Information technology. Developments in microcomputers, word processors, electronic mail systems and communication technology which have made possible the electronic office.

Ink jet printer. A printer that builds up characters and graphics out of patterns (matrices) of tiny blobs of ink squirted on the paper. The quality of print so produced is normally higher than that from dot-matrix printers.

Input device. A peripheral unit which allows data to be entered into a computer. Examples are a *light pen* and a *keyboard*.

Integrated circuit. A tiny chip of, usually, silicon which contains many electronic components.

Integrated package. A package usually combining a word processor, *database*, spreadsheet and communications program, sometimes with other applications.

Interactive. Describes a program or system that requires input from a user, to which the computer responds with output that may call for further input (ie almost any program apart from one where the user simply gazes at the screen).

I/O. Input/Output.

IT. *Information technology.*

Keyboard (computer). An inputting device, which has a standard (QWERTY) typewriter pattern with additional keys such as function keys, control and escape keys.

Kilobyte. One thousand *bytes* (actually 1024).

LAN. *Local area network.*

Laser printer. A printer that uses laser light to produce an initial photo image. Toner is applied to the paper by heat and pressure. Laser printers are faster and quieter than earlier types of printer like the *daisy wheel* or *dot matrix*, and generally produce print work of higher quality.

Light pen. An inputting device, usually for reading bar-codes.

Lisp. An acronym for list processing. Lisp is a high level language in which both programs and data are expressed as lists.

Local area network (LAN). Where a number of computers are linked together, usually in the same room or building (contrast with *wide area network).*

Loop. Instructions that are repeated until a set of criteria is satisfied.

Macro instruction. A source program instruction which, when translated, gives rise to several or many machine code instructions.

Magnetic disk. A direct access storage medium consisting of one or more flat circular disks, from which data can be retrieved directly without searching through other items of data which are not required.

Magnetic tape. A tape with a magnetisable layer on which data can be stored.

Megahertz (MHz). One million hertz. Measures speed of *CPU.*

Mainframe. A term used to distinguish large and powerful computers from the smaller minicomputers and microcomputers. They tend to have a very large backing store and a fast *CPU.*

Main memory. The memory of the computer which stores programs and data currently being run (processed by the *CPU*). When power is turned off the data is lost.

Megabyte. One million *bytes.*

Menu-driven program. A list of options presented by the computer. The user can make a selection from a menu by moving the cursor and then pressing the enter key, or by clicking on it with a mouse.

MICR. Magnetic ink character recognition. A machine that recognises characters printed in magnetic ink.

Microcomputer. Usually refers to a third-generation computer whose *central processing unit* is made up of a silicon chip which contains thousands of integrated microscopic electronic components housing the arithmetic and logic unit, plus the central unit. A small computer such as a PC.

Microprocessor. A *central processing unit* (CPU) or co-processor contained on a single chip.

Microsecond. One millionth of a second.

Millisecond. One thousandth of a second.

Minicomputer. A medium-size computer – bigger than a *microcomputer* but smaller than a *mainframe* computer.

MIP. An acronym for million instructions per second. This is a measure of *microprocessor* speed.

Modem. Modulator/Demodulator – a device that allows computers to communicate with one another via a telecommunication line.

Monitor. The screen on which information is displayed, more commonly known as *VDU* (visual display unit).

Mouse. A small hand-held device used for cursor control. Useful for selecting options (*icons*) in a *menu-driven program*.

Multi-user system. A system that allows several users to access the computer simultaneously.

Nanosecond. One thousand millionth of a second.

Network. A number of computers linked together, with the capacity to share computing power or storage facilities.

NLQ. Stands for near letter quality – refers to quality of printing.

Non-volatile memory. A storage medium that continues to hold data after power has been turned off, eg *ROM, PROM, EPROM*.

Off line. Not under the control of the central processor.

On line. Under the control of the central processor.

Operating system. A set of programs which supervise and control the general running of the computer.

Optical fibre. A very fine glass strand (like a wire) that allows data to be transmitted very quickly, using light signals.

Output device. A device such as a printer, that allows the computer to produce (output) information.

Overwriting. Where a data item is written over an existing data item, which as a result is erased. For example, if a file is saved using the same name as an existing file, the new file will be saved and the existing one will be erased.

Parallel processing. Here the computer instructions are executed in parallel. This requires a number of processors. Most computers have only one processor and execute instructions serially.

Pascal. A high-level structured programming language.

Password. A set of characters which must be presented to the computer before access is allowed either to the whole system or part of it.

Peripheral device. Items such as printers, *keyboards* etc, which can be connected to the *CPU*.

Picosecond. One million millionth of a second.

Programmer. A person who writes computer programs.

PROM. Programmable Read Only Memory (*ROM*).

Protocol. A standard set of rules for the exchange of data between two or more remote devices.

Pull-down menu. A facility whereby a user can 'pull' a menu down on to the screen by selecting an *icon* or a word from the top of the screen.

Query language. A language that allows users to make enquiries of a database.

RAM. Random access memory.

Record. A collection of related fields.

Response time. The time taken between a query at the keyboard and the computer's response on the screen.

ROM. Read only memory.

Scanner. A device which can convert text and graphics into computer readable form. For example a picture could be scanned, which could then be displayed on the *VDU*.

Scroll. When text either rolls up or down on the VDU. As each new line appears at the bottom of the screen, the lines at the top disappear one by one. Similar to credits at the end of a film.

Search. The scanning of data items according to specified criteria, eg all names beginning with the letter 'M'.

Simplex line. A data transmission line which allows data to be sent in one direction only.

Soft sectored. Refers to the way in which a disk has been formatted. Sectors are designated by information written on the disk by a program. The sectors can be altered.

Software. Programs of various types which can be run on a computer.

Sort. To arrange data in a particular order, eg alphabetically or numerically.

Syntax. The rules of grammar and structure governing the use of a programming language.

Syntax error. Where the rules are not followed correctly.

Systems analyst. A person specialising in systems analysis.

Systems software. Programs which are concerned with the running of the hardware and not with specific applications eg utilities, operating systems.

Telecommuting. A word that has come to mean that a worker does not have to travel to work, but is connected to the office or place of work via a computer terminal.

Utility. A program that performs tasks such as formatting or copying a *disk*.

VDU. Visual display unit – see *monitor*.

Verification. The act of ensuring that data transferred from source document to computer system is correct.

Virtual storage. Whereby the *backing store* is accessed, apparently, in the same way as the main store.

Virus. Code or codes hidden in a computer program with the intention of destroying data or corrupting the system.

Wide area network (WAN). Where computers are linked together by a telecommunications line over a long distance.

The link can be between offices in the same city, other cities or even other countries.

Wimp. Windows, *icons, mouse* and *pull-down menus.*

Winchester disk. A fixed disk drive in which a sealed unit houses the access arms and the magnetic disk. Also commonly referred to as a hard disk.

Worm. Write once, read many times.

Further Reading from Kogan Page

Great Answers to Tough Interview Questions, 3rd edition, Martin John Yate

How to Pass Graduate Recruitment Tests, Mike Bryon

How to Pass Selection Tests, Mike Bryon and Sanjay Modha

How to Pass Technical Selection Tests, Mike Bryon and Sanjay Modha

How to Win as a Part-Time Student, Tom Bourner and Phil Race

How You Can Get That Job!, Rebecca Corfield

Preparing Your Own CV, Rebecca Corfield

Successful Interview Skills, Rebecca Corfield

Test Your Own Aptitude, 2nd edition, Jim Barrett and Geoff Williams